Niagara

RICHARD BAIN

❖

Foreword by Donald Ziraldo

The BOSTON
MILLS PRESS

Published in 2000 by
BOSTON MILLS PRESS
132 Main Street
Erin, Ontario N0B 1T0
Tel 519-833-2407
Fax 519-833-2195
e-mail books@bostonmillspress.com
www.bostonmillspress.com

An affiliate of
STODDART PUBLISHING CO. LIMITED
34 Lesmill Road
Toronto, Ontario, Canada
M3B 2T6
Tel 416-445-3333
Fax 416-445-5967
e-mail gdsinc@genpub.com

Distributed in Canada by
GENERAL DISTRIBUTION SERVICES LIMITED
325 Humber College Boulevard
Toronto, Canada M9W 7C3
Orders 1-800-387-0141 Ontario & Quebec
Orders 1-800-387-0172 NW Ontario & other provinces
e-mail cservice@genpub.com

Distributed in the United States by
GENERAL DISTRIBUTION SERVICES INC.
PMB 128, 4500 Witmer Industrial Estates
Niagara Falls, New York 14305-1386
Toll-free 1-800-805-1083
Toll-free fax 1-800-481-6207
e-mail gdsinc@genpub.com
www.genpub.com

04 03 02 01 00   1 2 3 4 5

THE CANADA COUNCIL | LE CONSEIL DES ARTS
FOR THE ARTS | DU CANADA
SINCE 1957 | DEPUIS 1957

*We acknowledge for their financial support of our publishing
program the Canada Council, the Ontario Arts Council, and
the Government of Canada through the Book Publishing
Industry Development Program (BPIDP).*

CATALOGING IN PUBLICATION DATA

Bain, Richard (Richard G.), 1954–
Niagara

ISBN 1-55046-287-3

1. Niagara Peninsula (Ont.) — Pictorial works. I. Title.

FC3095.N5B34 2000   971.3'33804'0222   00-930502-5
F1095.N5B34 2000

Design by Gillian Stead

Printed and bound in Hong Kong
by Book Art Inc., Toronto

For Joan

The early morning sun illuminates the mist over Niagara.

Foreword

One of the most rewarding parts traveling the world as Canada's wine ambassador is coming home and appreciating the beauty and diversity of the Niagara region. When returning to my home at the winery, the route I take is the Niagara River Parkway, which hugs the cliffs and winds its way through flower gardens and forests. This drive was once described by Winston Churchill as "one of the prettiest drives on a Sunday afternoon."

There are other ways to arrive here. The first Welland Canal was constructed in 1829 to link Lake Erie with Lake Ontario so that ships could navigate further inland, bypassing the natural barrier presented by the Niagara Escarpment. The Bruce Trail capitalized on the Escarpment, and today its 480 miles (773 kms) of beautiful hiking trails lead thousands of hikers from Queenston Heights to Tobermory, at the northern tip of the Bruce Peninsula.

In 1878 Lord Dufferin, then Governor General of Canada, introduced the Niagara Falls Park Act for the preservation of the natural beauty of Niagara. This parkland now extends along the entire length of the Niagara River and accommodates golf courses, historic sites, the Niagara Parks School of Horticulture, the newly opened Butterfly Conservatory, world-class wineries, restaurants, inns, marinas, trails, vineyards, and so much more.

The trails at Niagara Glen Nature Area descend deep into the Gorge, revealing layers of rock laid down over four hundred million years ago. Many believe that the Niagara region was first inhabited over ninety thousand years ago by nomadic hunters who moved along the shores of Lake Erie. A Jesuit priest named Father Gabriel Lalemant recorded the Iroquois name for the river as *Onguiaahra*. One theory has it that *Onguiaahra* eventually came to be pronounced *Niagara*. Others have it that Niagara was a word used by the Neutral people to mean "Thunder of Waters."

About twelve thousand years ago that thunder of waters, Niagara Falls, the world's greatest waterfall as measured by volume, actually cascaded over the face of the Escarpment at Queenston. It has since eroded its way about seven miles (11 km) upstream, cutting through the Gorge at the rate of one foot every ten years, to reach the present location of the Horseshoe Falls.

Although only 35 miles (56 kms) long, the Niagara River is one of the world's foremost sources of hydroelectric power. This churning river provides enough force to generate 4.4 million kilowatts of power from the Sir Adam Beck Generating Station, in Canada, and the Robert Moses plant directly across the river in the United States, enough to illuminate twenty-four million hundred-watt lightbulbs.

At the mouth of the Niagara River is the historic town of Niagara-on-the-Lake, one of the best preserved early nineteenth-century towns in North America and home of the acclaimed Shaw Festival Theatre. The town played a significant role in the early government and commerce of the area, and was central to the outcome of the War of 1812. Today, the town is a tourist mecca, surpassed only by the Falls themselves.

It has been said that to understand the history of Niagara-on-the-Lake is to understand the history of early Ontario. The settlement was originally known as Butlersburg, for Colonel John Butler, and didn't become Niagara-on-the-Lake until the 1880s.

Another important military figure of the day, Major-General Isaac Brock is honored by the Brock Monument, which rises high atop the Escarpment at Queenston Heights.

Brock University also bears his name and is home to the Cool Climate Oeonology and Viticultural Institute.

The success of the Niagara wine industry has much to do with the land itself. This small, geographically distinct parcel of land is sheltered on the north by Lake Ontario, on the south by Lake Erie, on the east by the Niagara River, and on the west by the height of the Escarpment. This escarpment was the shoreline of pre-Ice Age Lake Iroquois, the massive single lake from which the present five Great Lakes were formed. North of the Escarpment is a flat plain. This area, on the first bench of land between the Escarpment and Lake Ontario, favors the growing of Vitis vinifera varieties of

Ripe for harvest. Niagara grapes produce some of the finest wines in the world.

grapes such as pinot noir and chardonnay, as well as other fruits, including peaches, cherries and apricots. The Niagara region is considered a cool viticultural area. The ability to produce high-quality mature fruit in summer and being blessed with cold winters enables us to produce our internationally renowned VQA icewines.

A practice row along the Henley in St. Catharines.

The Niagara region is a wonderful four-season destination that encompasses hundreds of attractions, but a great way to discover this region is to experience its regional foods and wines. They form an identifiable, original culinary style, one that reflects the land and its people. Gourmet chefs from both sides of the border make regular pilgrimages to the Niagara countryside to stock their kitchens with fruits and vegetables, the product of fine harvests. And as they leave, traveling down one of the world's most scenic parkways, the Niagara experience will stay with them until they next return.

From quaint towns to thundering waterfalls, fine inns to modern industry, historic pageantry to world-class wineries, Richard Bain has eloquently captured the Niagara region in the pages of this wonderful book.

Donald Ziraldo

*Built in 1864, the Prince of Wales Hotel in Niagara-on-the-Lake
has hosted Royalty and treats its patrons royally.*

One of the quaint bed-and-breakfasts in the "Old Town" of Niagara-on-the-Lake.

Ready to greet guests at the Queen's Landing Inn and Conference Resort overlooking the Niagara River.

The Preservation Fine Art Gallery features important works by

Trisha Romance, Alex Colville and Philip Craig.

OPPOSITE: *The Varey House, one of Niagara-on-the-Lake's*

beautiful early nineteenth-century homes.

At the end of the Niagara River

sits the Kiely Heritage Inn and Restaurant, built in 1832.

Spring blossoms in Niagara-on-the-Lake.

*Reflections through the window at the
Oban Inn. Flower gardens and wine —
a taste of Niagara.*

*The Oban Inn, built in 1824, burned to the
ground on December 25, 1992. It was
completely rebuilt and opened once again
for business in November of 1993.*

A great place to enjoy splendid food and fine wines, the Shaw Cafe Wine Bar.

OPPOSITE: *The marquee at the Shaw's Royal George Theatre.* The Cambridge Guide to Theatre *lists the Shaw Festival as "an annual summer festival in Niagara-on-the-Lake, Ontario, devoted to presenting the works of George Bernard Shaw and his contemporaries, and home to one of the finest acting ensembles in North America."*

The Royal George Theatre, one of three theatres that make up the Shaw Festival,

offering plays from April to November.

The Festival Theatre at "The Shaw."

Picture-perfect pickets around a home in Niagara-on-the-Lake.

OPPOSITE: *The old Niagara Apothecary, built in 1866,*
on Queen Street in Niagara-on-the-Lake.

*Looking out towards
Lake Ontario, this home,
built in 1835, was once
the Whale Inn, a hotel
for sailors.*

The Silly Old Bear Shop, with a young Christopher Robin

admiring authentic A. A. Milne classics.

Enjoying a sunset after a day of photographing with Dad.

The canon at Fort George pointed towards Fort Niagara on the U.S. side of the border,
reminds visitors of the battles that defined the geographical boundaries of our two countries.

OPPOSITE: *Raising the flag at the start of another peaceful day.*

*A lone maple tree
and grapevines after
the autumn harvest.*

Taking part in a tasting seminar at Hillebrand Estates Winery.

OPPOSITE: *Checking the progress of the wine at Hillebrand.*

*Inspecting the grapes prior to the
harvest at Inniskillin Winery.*

*Late autumn, with grapes left
on the vine for icewine.*

Early summer in the vineyards.

The Library Wine Cellar at Inniskillin Wines.

One of many magnificent estates
along the shores of Lake Ontario.

Bleak fields barren of summer's fruit.

Frozen grapes will be harvested for the making of Niagara's renowned icewines.

OPPOSITE: *Waiting for next season at Inniskillin.*

OVERLEAF: *Looking down the Niagara River towards Lake Ontario*
from a scenic lookout at Queenston Heights.

The Laura Secord homestead in Queenston Village. Secord set out from this location
to warn British forces of the impending attack at Beaverdams during the War of 1812.

McFarland House, built in 1800, was used as a hospital during the War of 1812.

Today it is a tea room with a beautiful period herb garden

and plays host to special events of living history.

The Brock Monument, high atop Queenston Heights, commemorates Major-General
Sir Isaac Brock, who lost his life in the decisive battle at Queenston during the War of 1812.

The Lewiston–Queenston Bridge.

The international border joins two countries long at peace with each other.

Dalhousie House, a seniors' recreation center
along the shore of the Henley in St. Catharines.

Peaches are a common sight at the numerous fruit stands found along the Niagara Parkway.

Fruit trees blossom with color as spring returns.

The Welland Canal joins Lake Ontario and Lake Erie

allowing ships to navigate around the Falls.

The churning Niagara River fuels the Sir Adam Beck Niagara Generating Station.

Autumn on the grounds of the
Niagara Parks Botanical Gardens
and School of Horticulture,
a 100-acre sanctuary that
promises a feast for the senses.

The 11,000-square-foot Niagara Parks Butterfly Conservatory
is home to thousands of butterflies representing 38 species.

*The plants on the face of Niagara's Floral Clock, designed and maintained by
the Niagara Parks Commission, are changed twice per season.*

The Whirlpool Golf Course, which winds its way along the Niagara Parkway,

is just one of the many fine courses in the region.

The Whitewater Boardwalk along the Niagara River.

The Great Gorge Adventure,

where spectators can observe the rapids rage just a few feet away.

*Niagara's famous Spanish Aero Car is an exhilarating
way to see the whirlpool from high overhead.*

The rainbow over the Horseshoe Falls is a familiar sight.

OPPOSITE: *The Niagara River and Parkway just before the Falls,*
as seen from the Minolta Tower.

The sun illuminates the water as it
cascades over the Falls, while a raincoated
visitor journeys through tunnels
150 feet behind the thundering waters.

At the helm of the Maid of the Mist VI, *Captain Fletcher maneuvers his vessel towards the base of the Falls.*

The Maid of the Mist *as it passes the American Falls. Spray and surging water make for a thrilling river cruise.*

During winter at Niagara, the mist from the Falls routinely coats nearby trees with ice.

*Niagara Falls at night. At left is the Skylon tower on the Canadian side
with the Rainbow Bridge spanning the river to New York State.*

OPPOSITE: *Fireworks can be seen over the Falls every Friday night
from May to September.*

The railing around "Table Rock".

Winter's artistry at Niagara.

Visitors in yellow raincoats go beneath Bridal Veil Falls to explore the Cave of the Winds.

OPPOSITE: *The American Falls as viewed from Goat Island.*

The Marriott Fallsview Hotel and the Minolta Tower.

OPPOSITE: *The statue "Freedom" at the entrance to the Niagara Parks Greenhouse.*
The greenhouse features a collection of plants and flowers of seasonal interest,
as well as a collection of tropical plants from around the globe.

One of the region's newest attractions, Casino Niagara, bills itself as
"Niagara's Other Natural Wonder" and is Canada's largest Vegas-style casino.

Taking care of "Neocia," a killer whale at Marineland.

OPPOSITE: *Clifton Hill shops, wax museums, restaurants and other attractions are to be found on "a street of fun."*

Queen Victoria Park,
a truly royal park
that blooms with acres
of colorful gardens,
fish ponds and
intriguing architecture.

Pampas grass alight with the sun's rays
along the Robert Moses Parkway near Lewiston.

Morning mist along the Niagara River near Fort Erie.

Two centuries of military history. Soldiers at Historic Fort Erie bring this recreated
1812 British garrison to life as they perform period re-enactments. Directly across the
Niagara River is the Buffalo and Erie County Naval and Military Park.

A hotdog vendor in Cathedral Park, in downtown Buffalo, awaits the lunchtime crowd.

OPPOSITE: *The Liberty Building is one of many examples*
of gothic architecture in downtown Buffalo.

The Niagara Power Project in Lewiston, New York,

supplies hydro-electric power to the northeastern United States.

Springtime "stateside" along the Robert Moses Parkway.

OVERLEAF: *A quiet morning anchorage near Grand Island, New York.*

Old Fort Niagara, located at the mouth of the Niagara River, in Youngstown,

was an American stronghold during the War of 1812.

The United States Coast Guard Station "Niagara," in Youngstown,
serves the Upper Niagara River and Lake Ontario.

OPPOSITE: Sailboats at the Niagara-on-the-Lake Sailing Club await their crews.

Time out from a carriage ride in Niagara-on-the-Lake.

OPPOSITE: *The Oban Inn's dining room*
overlooks the Niagara River and Lake Ontario.

Snowfall at the Prince of Wales Hotel, with carriages waiting for their next passengers.

OPPOSITE: *The Niagara Historical Museum on Castlereagh Street in Niagara-On-The-Lake.*

A lamp post covered in ice from winter storms along the Niagara River.

An old horse-drawn carriage in front of the Pillar and Post Inn, Spa and Conference Centre.

The Pillar and Post was formerly a fruit cannery, built in the late 1890s.

Autumn along the Niagara River, with Old Fort Niagara visible on the American side.

Solitude. Overlooking the river just a few miles from the thunder of the Falls.

Acknowledgements

SO MANY TIMES I took visitors to the Falls and said I had been to "Niagara." But I missed so much. Now, after spending a year photographing this wonderfully diverse region, I realize that it is truly a treasure for both Canadians and Americans alike. What struck me the most was the beauty of each season — from the graceful latticework of ice-coated trees in winter, to the crackle of dry vines underfoot in late fall, to warm summer afternoons spent enjoying the fruits of the vintner's labor in a quaint inn.

So many people assisted in the creation of this book. A very heartfelt thank you to Donald Ziraldo, a legend in the Canadian wine industry and a major reason that Niagara wines have rightfully become world-renowned; to Deborah Pratt from Inniskillin Wines; to George Bailey, Sarah Finch, and the staff of the Niagara Parks Commission; to Christopher Newton and Odette Yazbeck from the Shaw Festival; Ron Dale from Fort George; and Jim Hill from Historic Fort Erie. Thanks also to Rachael Savio, Niagara-on-the-Lake Vintage Inns; Claudia Reis, Konzelmann Estate Winery; Ann Marie Rondinelli and Dawn Oscvirk, Marineland of Canada; Penny Taylor, Minolta Tower; Sherri Lockwood, Hillebrand Estates Winery; Jennifer Cebado, Niagara-on-the-Lake Chamber of Commerce and Visitor & Convention Bureau; the Greater Buffalo Convention & Visitors Bureau; Fran Lavigueur, Niagara County Tourism; and Emil Bende and Capt. Jerry Fletcher, Maid of the Mist Corporation. Also, special thanks to Philip Lapidus and Kodak Canada for their assistance.

I am amazed at how a manuscript of transparencies is transformed into a book of this caliber. John Denison, Noel Hudson and Gillian Stead from the Boston Mills Press have done an outstanding job.

To my wife, Joan, and our children, Caroline, Daniel, Brett and Jordan, thank you for putting up with me while I spent so much of our family time "in Niagara, taking pictures." I do remember all the trips that we were able to make together, and I hope that our time together was as memorable for you as it was for me.

Finally, to all the people of Niagara, on both sides of the river, thank you for sharing this beautiful region with me, and ultimately with all who see it in the pages of this book.

Richard Bain